More

Linda Carney-Goodrich has su̶c̶
difficult. Many survivors of chi̶
Carney-Goodrich turns her men̶o̶r̶i̶e̶s̶ ̶i̶n̶t̶o̶ ̶p̶o̶w̶e̶r̶f̶u̶l̶,̶ ̶r̶e̶l̶a̶t̶a̶b̶l̶e̶,̶ ̶b̶r̶i̶l̶l̶i̶a̶n̶t̶
poems. She has retained a sense of humor. Her imagery is striking. Her
depiction of the use of religion to control and punish a child is particularly
strong. She has come out the other side as victorious.
— **Marge Piercy**, author of *On The Way Out, Turn Off The Light*

"Each night I send the messages tied to / pigeon feet or auburn strands of hair
/ like bows back to the girl I once was / She will only get the ones I remember
to send." The fearless speaker in Linda Carney-Goodrich's *Dot Girl* is "the
family watchman," an apologist for how the sins of fathers, mothers, and
siblings, secular and religious systems, need not be passed wholly onto the
daughter. But there is no full escape from the original secrets and sins held
by those who came before. Each poem in this stunning collection echoes
down decades, reverberates to the bone – liturgy for a body processing
trauma. It unfolds the terrible beauty of confessions made for more than
survival, prayers built on hope in a possible, promised future.
— **Matthew E. Henry**, author of *The Third Renunciation*

Dot Girl is a lyrical confession. Linda Carney-Goodrich's poems are
enactments of her world laid bare. "There are stories that became parts / of
the body with rooms of their own", each poem carrying a don't-mess-with
/ been-messed-with, hard-hitting, heartbreaking, from-the-hip tone that'll
make any reader hooked on her narrative. Carney-Goodrich transcends
what torments her by giving diagnosis to what has been undiagnosed. This
collection has the voice of determination, a poet transcribing her self-
portrait as merciless Boston staggers to be more than her backdrop. Though
in the end, it is the poet who takes you to every edge.
— **Alexis Ivy**, author of *Taking the Homeless Census*

Linda Carney-Goodrich breaks new ground in this story of redemption
and transformation. The poet takes us by the hand and guides us through
her childhood, coming of age in Boston and surviving foster care. In these
poems we take flight, move through bracing sea water, experience clouds,
amidst violence and abuse. We see the world through the eyes of a child
who refuses to be broken, we visit the landmarks of the poet's childhood:
the parks and streets of Dorchester. Growing up in Catholic Boston, amidst
abuse, poverty, and misogyny, Linda confronts the past, stares it down and
helps us "glimmer in the knowing." These empowering poems make me feel
braver and show how "we call each other home."
— **Deborah Leipziger**, author of *Story & Bone*

DOT GIRL

LINDA CARNEY-GOODRICH

Nixes Mate Books
Allston, Massachusetts

Library of Congress Control Number: 2024932022

ISBN 978-1-949279-53-5

Nixes Mate Books
PO Box 1179
Allston, MA 02134
nixesmate.pub

"In trying to heal the wound that never heals, lies the strangeness."
— Federico García Lorca

"When poets go back by way of memory and imagination to past traumas
to engage or re-engage them, then those poets are taking control – are
shaping and ordering and asserting power over the hurtful events. In
lyric poems, they're both telling the story from their point of view and
also shaping the experience into an order (the poem) that shows they
have power over what (in the past) overpowered them."
— Gregory Orr, *Primer for Poets*

CONTENTS

DOT GIRL

We move in fog in reek of fish,
sneaking out screen-less windows at night,
climbing down garage roofs or window-tapping trees.

In slick shiny streets under faint blue light,
we dance in silence to the beach.
The bosses and their workers snore through the perfect time.

We scream our names like angry owls under the bridge by the beach.
Your brother slept here, where the tunnel curves by the road.
One night he saw us, he was singing the Rolling Stones.

Knees winked from the holes in his filthy white pants.
Car lights flashed him a spotlight of shame.
We pretended not to hear him say, *Get outta here.*

The sand is sharp, but we go barefoot.
Tiny pieces of glass prick our feet reminding us of pain we haven't felt.
The air, foul and alive as we strip down under each other's starlike eyes.

The two of us back float, white stick bodies in bruised and murky water.
Only hands touching, we breathe out the memories of the day,
stare at celestial light born before we were.

You claim there is a spot where the water meets the sky,
where souls swim free and no one calls them home.
In the morning, we sneak back to wake our parents.
Remind them to take us to school.

DORCHESTER BIKE RIDE
(VODKA, BEER, AND CIGARETTES)

I swim in the beach with green glass sand.
Go to school with the saints of Boston, do crafts
with the Girl Scouts. Everyone knows girls
don't build campfires, don't rough it like boys.

I wonder at the woman who swam the English Channel.
How was it that she knew she could do that?
I wonder if God loves me, why did he make me so ugly?
Why did he make me a left-handed girl?

I ride my bike on Salina Road with my eyes closed.
Smell the boiled Sunday dinners.
Wonder what it is to fly
to jump from cloud to cloud.

Vodka, beer and cigarettes.
Essential as coffee,
Make me a screw driver!
Go down the stoah and get me a carton Pall Malls!

Will I need the things adults need?
The blackness of it scares me.
I shake my Magic Eight Ball:

The future is uncertain.
I play the *Woman's Gotta do What a Woman's Gotta Do Game*
with my blood sister, Mary.
We wait in our clubhouse longing to hear Mayor White say,
No schools in all schools in Boston!

Mary shows me a dirty magazine.
She tells me, *One day this is going to happen to you.*
I ride my bike with my eyes closed.
I've dreamt so many times I can fly, I believe it is my secret power.

I ride my bike from stop sign to stop sign to streetlight to school yards
to parking lots, connecting my own private constellations.
My father gives my mother a haircut to save his hard earned money.
He cuts her hair so short, she needs a wig.

I go to church. I take communion,
wonder what would happen if
I secretly hide the body of Christ in my coat pocket,
sneak it home and plant it like a seed in my yard.

If I grew wings, they'd sprout hot pink and blue.
But in my dreams of flying, I don't have any wings.
I fly naked in the sky, doing tricks.
No one can touch me.

Look! Look! It's a girl in the sky! They would marvel.
That is special, cause girls don't sit with Christ.
Girls can't be priests.
Girls don't get to keep their own last names.

I swim two hours a night hoping my father will be asleep when I get home.
I spend so many hours staring up at the sky.
My third-grade teacher told me that clouds don't feel like anything,
but I know she's not that smart.

Of course, clouds feel like something. Clouds feel like cotton.
Like sticky taffy. They feel like water or a mattress.
They feel like a tight hug from Aunt Irene with the sweet,
boozy breath and the big, fluffy boobs.

Complex Post-Traumatic Stress Disorder

A psychological state induced by prolonged psychosocial trauma, often in early childhood, coupled with disempowerment and inability to escape.

TIME TRAVEL

Certain of imminent annihilation
unceasing bracing retracing,

correct mistakes before they are found

shudder each day growing

you know you can fly swim in air

bionic eyes ears nose high alert day night

God tests you like Job to find out if he can love you

his great thumb over head

ready to crush extinguish

it will always find   anywhere you are

discover a way escape the body

disappear into air   travel back and forth

in time like a rocking chair

I meet you there

Each night I send the messages
tied to pigeon feet or auburn strands of hair
like bows back to the girl I once was

She will only get the ones I remember to send

There in the welfare apartment, the lead paint chipping,
the second hand crib, a futon used as a bed,
a dining table with ornate legs saved from sidewalk trash
She could have sold it for something
except for the burn, inch deep over half the surface

She is there back then seeking out of body experiences
and a parachute for the baby

Take care of this one I tell her in my best goddess voice
Look after her

I see her hover above her body

The red sheets form a blood swaddle
Except for brief excursions, there is no escape from the body
The men flash with their keys and tools
hands and eyes

hands and eyes and stomachs
The women with their judgement
The children with their hungry mouths,
their bell like laughter,
their soft and endless need

I tell her, *You are not your youth, your usefulness, your breast milk.
Don't mistake yourself.*

Soul Friend, the only one I truly know. I am bound to you.

I am the needle of your golden thread.

Coming home from school, dread tight on my shoulders like a coat.

Sunday dinners, how she'd cut half gallons of ice cream in slices
to make it feed twelve of us.

Government cheese, brand-less canned food,
white labels and black words that read simply: Beans, Corn, Peas.

My brother telling me he was my sister.

My other brother telling him only wimps wanted to be weather men.

Lying on the cool ground staring at the clouds for hours with no
boredom or impatience.

Hiding under water in the Murphy pool believing no one could see me.

Fighting all afternoon at Garvey Park. Surrounded by girls I punched –
Michelle Ball, in the face until she had an asthma attack,
Ann Marie McDougal, til her nose bled hot all over my hand,
Nancy Connell, til she cried and I realized they'd let me go home.

Competing in the Little Miss Dorchester contest. Losing
in the picture drawing segment.

My sister peeing her pants laughing on the Fourth of July
when dad locked us out of the house.

Wondering why I was alive.

That naked moment in Park Street Station
when my mother claimed she no longer loved me.

Swimming like I can fly through water.

Being beaten in the tub. Being held down under the water.

The postman always smiling, always friendly, then one day gone.

My neighbors' puppies, the urge I had to put them in the dryer.

Lying in the burning snow thinking about turning seven,
how soon I'd have two digits,
how soon I would be old.

My mother crying at her own mother's grave.

The sting of her fingers and her fists on my back.

Waiting with the social worker for my parents to arrive,
relieved when they don't.

Her lipstick on Kleenex and cigarettes, picking them up and hiding them
like I somehow had stolen a kiss.

Thank you for wearing denim vests and scally caps to class.
You looked like a Boston Kenny Rogers.
The scent of smoke and what I came to know later as scotch
lingered about you, warm as bread.
Poetry teacher, thank you for making my mother want
to leave the house again.
You gave me poems I would not have known.
They were my violet incantations, my lonely dreams, my only friends.
Thank you for making places I could escape to
where Hope is a bird, daffodils dance.
There is a burning Tyger in the forest of my heart, still.
Did I ever tell you how I dreamt my mother would take me
and we would run away with you?
I just knew you'd have a big house with shelves bending
from the weight of all those books,
quiet with golden cushions and fancy water.
Dear poetry guy, I forget your name. What was it?
Thank you for reciting my grandfather's
poem about his time in Deer Island Prison.
My mother bought me my first new dress,
all white with little pink roses, tied at my shoulders.
She put my hair up like a TV model, let me wear cherry lip gloss.
Oh, we looked good that day at Government Center.
I recited *Pudding Stone Shoes* into a microphone.

My soul crackled like it would split out my chest.
Poets are VIP's, you said.
Oh how the poems made me hum.
All those afternoons when I could've been fighting other girls
in the schoolyard til my shins bled, but instead
I went to find you.

I remember the day my father punched your face in.
We kids were all watching over the banister.
We laughed.
The story went that you came without calling,
to catch Dad at his worst.
You loved seeing him that way.
You pretended that you came to see us,
because it was Christmas and you had presents.
I wondered what they were.
Imagined crisp wrapping paper and bows.
Just for a moment, I hoped you would win.
Take the ten of us out into the night.
Somehow we'd all fit in your big black car.
How it would smell like Aunt Mary's Wind Song.
We'd drive off into the night, swim in your pool.
I can picture your hair, shiny with Vitalis.
A cleaner version of my father,
you wore a tie for nothing.
You did not drink screwdrivers.
Your kids did not know how to make them.
Your wife thought she was pretty in her makeup and fancy clothes.
Oh how we loved to make fun of you two!
We loved it the day Dad punched your face in.
Really we did.

We loved that we never had to see you see us again.
How did it happen that you had a car?
That your kids were clean and had nice clothes?
How exactly was it that you wore a black suit and shiny shoes,
while my Dad in bare feet and underwear strained
to knock your teeth out onto our kitchen floor?

Dissociation

A psychological defense mechanism in which specific, anxiety-provoking thoughts, emotions, or physical sensations are separated from the rest of the psyche. A defense mechanism the brain uses to cope with trauma. Often described as an "out of body" experience.

CHILDHOOD ROOMS

float like magenta and electric blue dust dots

    forget skin borders

laugh at things no one sees

mummified alive

stuck and staring and staring

mind wanders into turrets towers brambles

the Thicket

getting hit and hit   not feeling you

watch from the long corridor

chorus of voices colors swirled like softserve

dad scares all the clowns in the circus

ma is God's enforcer.

sin is to say it   sin is to know

fear invades cells like the kids' forks in birthday cake

shame stores memories in attics belly basements trunks boxes

stories tunnel in like worms

THE ROOMS OF THE BODY AT 3AM

There are stories that became parts

of the body with rooms of their own

They keep lost records in lockboxes

preserve the howling

in tightly sealed jars lining basement walls

register covert details in timeworn diaries

In floods sometimes an unruly belly button

or recalcitrant nipple will let out a scream

that vibrates through the body jolts

the brain awake at 3 AM emergency

pay attention   get the microscope

find the sin confess before

day light extinguishes the knowing   say the incantation

I am unworthy

say the word say the word I shall be healed

braid the stories tell me again

It's ok now. We're awake.

about the time you woke eight months pregnant with a giant
baby Huey-like man sitting watching, eyes silent plums
no questions and no explanation. He stood, his head just
about scraping the ceiling. Soundless floating.
You screamed inward, hoping to not wake the baby.
He does that sometimes.
The woman who housed you spoke it plain.
Do not be upset.

about the bolt on the bedroom door the foster lady showed
you how to use otherwise you'd be gotten, too.
Your bunkmate, a black-haired
queen teen dropout whose cutout underpants had a dangling
whistle for while they work she said she was pregnant
but was not the next Virgin Mother, silly.
Mary didn't like it.
She only said let it be done.

about the burn, the embers, the cigarette extinguished on your scalp,
the relief
of it finally happening. Natalie's teeth tearing into your arm,
the doctor's moon eyed disbelief that a dog had done it.
What of the cold grey bath water used by four before you?
What of how your mother licked her chops as you passed?
The rooms of the body, the shame it holds,
just to stand, just to walk, just to breathe.
Those wrists that need cover. The ear holes, too.
The belly button threatens to open and swallow you.

Body be whole, body be not ruined, body be safe, body be not ruined.

A mantra to counter the ruin within. The mantra to solve
the problem of existing a dangerous body.

The body remembers it all without the words to the story,
reminds you in the night, wakes you.

Pay attention! Express the milk,
wrap us tight like a mummy, douse the pain spots.
Don't sleep. Don't die.

Each Night My Mother
hands me a magnifying glass
We examine my sins like fingerprints
We count them like the stars

MY MOTHER'S EYES WERE BIRDS

Sometimes they were shy chickadees and others, violent chickens,
scared, angry, constantly pecking.
Oh, there were buzzard days and seagull days,
when her eyes cried themselves in two purple whirlpools swirling
slow   sad   circles in the skies of our dingy kitchen.

On blue jay days she fought ghosts in the living room,
worm catching days when she wore a robin's red apron.
Got things done.   Cleaned house. Scoured children.

Then there were ostrich days she fluttered through the house
to her own awkward rhythms. She wore short skirts, drew
faces of men and women on her knees and thighs.
See how they dance, she chirped.
I absorbed her calls and flight patterns.

My sister said my mother's true eyes were hiding,
that they had once beamed blue like a queen's heart.
I searched for them in the filthy pockets of her housecoats,
the jewelry box where she kept little nests of our auburn hair.
I yearned to hold them in my hands, to wear them like gems,
to glimmer in her knowledge and wither with her stare.

IN THE LIVING ROOM:
PANTOUM FOR A BROTHER

My mother tells my Brother
to breathe.
Her blade is sharp
pressed to his throat.

To breathe
I rock a strange rhythm.
Pressed to his throat
my feet don't touch the floor.

Back and forth I rock a strange rhythm.
Mother is screaming.
my feet don't touch the floor.
Big Brother limp like when Duke died.

My mother is screaming,
I won't pay for another damn ambulance.
Big Brother limp like when the dog played dead
her knife pressed to his throat.

I won't pay for another damn ambulance.
I'll kill you if you don't breath.
Her knife pressed to his throat.
I'm frozen like when I watch TV.

I'll kill you if you don't breathe.
I hear myself tell myself, *It's ok, it's ok, it's ok,*
frozen stuck like watching TV.
How will the doctor come, if nobody calls?

It's ok. it's ok, it's ok.
Mother's eyes scared like birds.
How will the doctor come, if nobody calls?
She tells me, *You didn't see this. You didn't see a thing.*

Mother's eyes scared birds.
Her blade is sharp.
You didn't see this. You never saw a thing,
my mother tells my Brother.

THE NIGHT MY BROTHER TOLD ME

In the dull, airy night I walked with my brother
on the pivotal eve of a transitioning star sign
his skin was stretching him into the other
a werewolf in morning surprised to find

the pivotal eve of a transitioning star sign
he was returned to himself again
a werewolf in morning surprised to find
the waxing and waning of our family men

when he returned to himself again
I urged him to fight as if he had a choice about
the waxing and waning cycles of our family men
he spat, gnashed teeth, and began to shout

I urged him to fight as if he had a choice about
the six inches he grew, the mallets his hands had become
he spat, gnashed teeth, conjured the voices,
blended ghosts of fathers and uncles crying as one

with the half foot he grew, the mallets his hands had become
in the dull, airy night I walked with my brother
ghosts of our fathers and uncles cried out as one
he fought his own body becoming some one other

MY BROTHER THOUGHT IT WAS FUNNY

to call his friends before carousing and have me sing into the phone,
You lush, you lush, you lush, you laaa-ush!
They called him Spook.

When he raced he'd be dead last until the end
then glide past everyone to gold.
Sing it, Lin! Sing the Stones! I'm shattered! I'm in tatters.

He'd slap on his Brut, saunter out to the street.
I knew the time was coming. God might have warned me.
My nimble eyes scan out the front door

seeking the first flake of snow
that I just know will get school canceled,
or the vampire I'll get to kill with my blue plastic cross.

I am on lookout. I am the family watchman.
Green dark hugs the street with her wet breath.
Street lights are UFOs, haloes, or shields.

His eyes emerge from the night,
two shades of blue, two knives of gray.
They fly like birds out his body onto our front porch.

My brother's face, unfamiliar. His nose is pressed
against the glass against mine pressed on the other side.
They're coming! Let me in!

But my parents told me to keep the door locked.
My brothers' monsters are invisible,
but we both know they are there.

He's locked out. I'm locked in.
I know it's true there's a monster in me, too
and in the street and in our house.

I'm a demon. I'm an angel.
I'm a future virgin mother in white.
I have visions and I know it before it happens.

My brother's hand breaks the glass in slow motion.
We're shattered in the hall on the 70's linoleum.
Pieces of us float forever in a story he won't recall and I never get right.

Shards of gold, splinters of green cling to my nightgown,
blood washes my toes, his arm hamburger,
the deepest cut I ever saw

yet my face, still whole as a miracle.

MOTHER'S DAY

Poured vodka into the vinegar bottles
peeled potatoes for twelve each night
Mother with her milk white teeth
her unavailable curves
cooking without aprons
made curtains from old towels
red lipstick bleeding
Scowled Mother-
twisted her eyebrows up into each other
Accused Mother-
knew her daughters made boys do awful things
Covered us and kept us dirty
Mother pounded loaves with a steady hand
sang to Sinatra and Perry Como
sprayed Wind Song in the air, on her wrists, on the dog
had boobs bigger than your head
moved slow, hit hard
mama laughed Joan Crawford
dared you to look her in the purple eye
Just once
Mama created all that you are
gave you her everything
You took it
Washed your sheets

made you cakes
that strawberry one with the strawberriest icing
You never did thank her for it
Mama knew what good wives do and good wives don't
Every supper was the last supper
Reeked resentment and chicken grease
Never stopped
reminding you that abortion was a sin
and she could have been a model.

MAMA HAD TEN BABIES AT SAINT MARGARET'S

Not in a litter in one day like a dog birthing puppies,

but like a woman year upon year with no choice.

My beautiful mother, what you might have been.

I heard the story from before I was born.

How you carefully dressed your five children,

tucked your dark hair beneath your lemon kerchief,

went out the front door with an old suitcase,

walked round the block,

came home and cried. And cried.

You saw that decrepit priest who said,

Go home. Be a good wife.

Was it cold that day?

Were you home before he was?

Did you make his dinner that night, not say a single word?

You were thirty seven when I was born.

Thirty seven with nine children and nothing of your own,

not a dime, not a room, not one cell.

It's a trick. Like a blinking light

there not there, there not there

We never see ourselves blinking

eyes closed 10% of waking hours

Like closed eyes that can still see, zero is a great contradiction

My father would punch my brothers' heads in rhythm to his words

You're a zero and you'll always be a zero

How can you be nothing and take up space?

How can you be both valuable and worthless?

Zero made steam come out my ears in third grade

My questions turned the teacher's face perplexed purple

You do this to me on purpose! You do this on purpose!

She shook my arm, slammed my desk against the wall

Was she as confused about zero as I was?

How can it make ten when you add it to one?

Does it hide infinity in its big fat roundness?

Do you know the secret?

Teach it to me.

THE GREEN SPARKLY DRESS

Hiding in the toy barrel, you choke on your own breath,
listen out for your father. His laughter wings through the night.

Once he said he pictured you in a Volkswagen beetle
driving to BU, said you looked like a model.

You wonder if anyone will discover you
waiting for him to sleep,

you in that green dress, the one worn by five sisters.
My Heart Belongs to Daddy glitters red across the chest.

You could tap dance on his bar. Bounce your curls. Laugh your eyes.
Tomorrow, you will wear that dress to school,

show Mrs. Handwell and the boys that you belong to someone.
But you will punch Paul Ryder in the jelly bean eye,

in the stupid eye when he tries to look up your dress.
For once you will be in the center of the circle.

The teacher will correct you. The children in unison will chide,
Keep your hands to yourself!

It is forbidden to tell
how your father's fist
pounded
his sons' skulls. Do not utter
the tale of your maroon shirt,
the one you buried in the yard.
I have sinned, Father, I know
being human means sinning.
But which sins are evil?
which sins are life, worms in mud,
viruses, gut bacteria?
Or something else entirely,
UFO or alien abductions?
How to know if when you left the body,
someone else showed up.
Whose sins are they, then?
Who should be the one to confess?

IF I COULD TIME TRAVEL,
I WOULD VISIT MY FATHER

He told me about the first time. He woke up
in the back of U-Haul drunk at 6 AM.
He was seventeen and it happened again and again.
The bottle inserted itself into his hands,
downed itself his throat. For decades,
it poured itself into clear bottles,
packed itself into his lunchbox at the post office.
It memorized his zip codes.

If I were permitted, I would time travel.
Go visit my father in the U-Haul, before he is a man.
If I could go as I am now, all middle aged and fearless,
I could look at him like he might be my son.
I can see him as my son, I can
touch his shoulder before it all goes worse.
In this pivotal moment I'd return, a great mother,
like a god disrupting tides.

I sometimes imagine I can will myself there,
cure the family illness, wake him, disrupt the repeat.
Is it useless to dream of being a god or shaman?
Can I love without forgiveness?
It must count for something, this vision in its amber light,

that I can visit anytime. Replay, rebuild the story.
Be the sunlight grasping through the dingy window.
Make it be love, the star to wake us.

Religious Abuse

administered under the guise of religion, including harassment or humiliation that may result in psychological trauma, can be perpetuated by religious leaders or other members of a religious community. Examples include using religious teachings to justify abuse, enforcing strict religious rules and practices that are harmful, shaming or ostracizing individuals who do not conform to religious norms, using religious authority to manipulate or control others, and denying basic needs in the name of religion. Religious abuse can have serious and long-lasting effects on individuals and communities, including trauma, emotional distress, and loss of faith.

Ceaselessly scan
for sins, devil desires,

confess to moon and stars, to priest,
to parents, admit the exact nature

terror of daylight, of shaking hands
or being seen, of the black marks

that obscure your soul
scour, scrub raw,

wash, confess, wash, confess,
you could die, but hell is waiting,

remember not to love
is a sin. A mortal sin.

Do you know all the sins?
The venial and the deadly?

Which thoughts are sins?
What is sloth, what is only resting, can you tell?

The God who made you is always watching
keeping lists immortal.

He is the one who knows.

LET'S ALL SIN, SAINT ANN'S, NEPONSET 1976

There was a bumper sticker all over the neighborhood
electric blue with a white cross
Let's All SIN

I was learning the sins of sloth and greed
Were you lazy or only tired, covetous or just hungry?
God knew

He'd be the one to send boils and locusts, transform
water of life into blood
I readied for his strike. What if he got it wrong?

When might he set the whole neighborhood ablaze, kill each firstborn?
I played Joan of Arc
tree branch as my sword, Big Wheel as my steed

A neighbor boy snapped my stick
Duh, you're a girl. You burn in the end.

The cross winked out at me from neighbors' windows.
I feared vampires, knew the cross could kill.
What was this secret code?
The SIN sticker with the cross went up at my house.

I knew about the blood of the lamb on doors so God
wouldn't kill the good people inside
but wouldn't he know good people
without being told?

I asked my mother, who taught me both to love and fear.
Light flashed a wicked storm in her
blue marble eyes. Her voice flitted with frightful pleasure
laughed rhythmic bells, each HA a bellow

Glory to God in the Highest and Peace to his people on Earth...

My mother's unvarnished face
in need of protection, makeup or mask.
I shook in my Mary Janes, I dared,
Why is everyone saying, let's all sin, when God doesn't want us to sin?
Would God ask me to fight my own mother?

Don't be an idiot. It doesn't mean to sin. It stands for something.
Let's all SIN. Stay in Neponset.

Terror flooded me, an ant in a jar my brothers would fill with water.
I heard of men and boys
in the night smashing windows of new black neighbors.
Saw on the news:

a white man clutching an American flag, lunging at a black man, as if to
stab him with the sharp
point of the flagpole
a brown girl's hair set on fire at school

My mother's eyes dug into mine, needles
pinning me in the patchwork

She told me of the planning, the SIN meetings at St. Ann's.
How to know if you have the right god

What if the monsters are the ones who feed you?
Maybe this was one of his sneaky, little tests

We aren't going to let them have our neighborhood.
My mother and God melded. Creator destroyer provider.
Do you get it, Linda? We stay together and keep them out.
Tell me you get it.

God's inconsumable inferno blazed in her eyes
Now is the time for the burning.
Behold, someone
floating in the lava core of my mind said
the time of the Lord is at hand.
I closed my useless lids against the infection. *Yes, I get it Ma.*

SISTER, WHY MUST OUR
SAVIORS BLEED FOREVER?

The sisters insisted Christ's wounds never heal.
He is bleeding still in heaven. They told me,
if I died wearing the scapula that was blessed by a priest,
I'd go straight to heaven with the god who takes virgins,
turns women to salt for glancing back
as their villages burn by his holy fire.
The scapula I wore in third grade
was blessed by a priest who molested my brother.
The Devil they taught me was worse than God.
Both never die, both wait forever and make me choose.
How to know, at 8 years old, that beautiful round
number of infinity, long past 7, the age of reason,
how to get away from god and all he created.
Does the fire in hell truly burn eternal?
Is my brother's priest there? Will I be?
It's a sin to doubt and to ask wrong questions.
But tell me, do you know, is this true, how I feel?
The torment churns through generations eats suffering and me
with my original wound covered by skin so thin all my light gets out.

CLOSEST TO GOD

Pope John Paul II arrives in Boston in his fancy, roofless car

close to Tinean Beach, where Bulger buries bodies

under the sharp rocks we call, *sand*, where we kids

sweat like dogs, our tongues panting for bomb pops.

His pope-wave renders the crowd silent as church.

The Vicar of Christ is debonair in his white cape and rubied fingers.

As his ride slows, I pray he'll throw us bits of candy and gold.

He meets my stare, his eyes, sapphire knives cutting away all that isn't
mine.

I picture my family like ants crushed beneath his wheels.

He was removed, released
back into the community.
The Cardinal was aware.
No one else was told,
not the police or his own family.
He was reassigned with little supervision.
Records were kept, records were sealed.
The Cardinal was informed.
It happened again.
He was removed, then reassigned.
His sister wrote he was bringing teens to his home.
Mahan asked to be defrocked,
I'm a sleaze. My disease runs so deep I can't be trusted.
He was removed, then reassigned,
received no oversight,
ran Boy Scouts, Legion of Mary,
summer camp, two grades of school.
A twelve year old jumped off his boat,
swam to shore to escape.
The police asked questions.
They were deflected.
They said they respected
the workings of the church.
He was removed, reassigned.

No one told the families.
He molested his own nephews.
In 1976 a second grade student
told a nun, who twisted her arm,
Never say anything like that again.

*A found poem. Source: *Boston Globe Spotlight Investigation. Priest abuse case eluded Law's reforms.* by Michael Rezendes, 2/19/2002

God, if what some say about you is true,
  you love me.
If what others say is true,
  you hate me.

I am a scorpion who stings itself.
I am only what a creator programmed me to be.
I am unable to escape my nature.
If a God can create things to hate, why shouldn't it be me?

Oh, the funny excuses a God can have to hate,
like where you put your genitals,
going to other Gods' houses,
dying before you get baptized.

I am on the long ago platform of Park Street Station.
The social worker comes to take me to a new home.
My mother fixes herself into my eyes
  saying goodbye.

I lost all the love I ever had for you, she tells me.
It has never been found.
What does it matter if no God loves me,
when I don't believe in God?

Being alive could be enough.

Before you knew shame,
you were a sunflower laughing to the sky.
You did not know anything was wrong
about the forest of your body.

In the garden of perpetual unmarked time
and ceaseless bounty,
you were cast out for learning
what your creator wanted hidden.

Forged people he could punish and chasten.
Made you to sin, so he could find you out.
He couldn't wait to sully your soul
with his little black marks.

You were formed to be found fault with.
Shroud yourself.
Legs the length of buildings,
hair in the wrong places,
a body, despite billows of garments,
marks you girl.

You know the loss of the great minds,
theft of their accomplishments,

the silencing. You know
they annihilated all your mothers,

removed them from their own bodies.
Try to learn their names,
knowing you could be killed for knowing,
how do apples taste and what is this part of my body for?

You stood before your earthly father,
doing dishes in the kitchen, while mother put other children to bed.
He made you, you know.
You belong to him like a shoe.

You must solve the problem of earning your exile.
See mother burrow under blankets,
betraying you with each held breath.
The virgin had to say *Father let it be done.*

Many say it so they won't be killed,
to become a martyr
or the next virgin mother.
Father let it be done,

to me and my daughters
and my grandmothers and theirs,
and theirs again and again and again.
You must know of the miraculous products that tear off skin and hair,

remove all traces of what is objectionable,
appear less threatening.
Scour yourself like a potato.
And you must like this.

Say you like this,
your place of honor.
Your body contains truths you can't recall,
aches memories your mind cannot decipher.

You must burn the books of your body,
hold the knowing inside
an invisible host, a planted seed
a weary treasure.

I planted a communion wafer in my front yard.
A grand tree erupted the very next day
with thick and tangled branches.
Tiny gods sprouted in place of leaves.
At first, they were all happy and singing songs.
Some hummed, some sang high, others did a little oompa, oompa.
A few of them bellowed great calls of OOOHHHHMMMMMM!

Mostly, it was perfect for three days, which seemed three hundred years.
Then some of them started screaming.
Don't do this, don't do that, they warned passersby.
Cars slowed down. Dogs barked. A priest came to question.
The mail carrier asked, *mind, if I pluck one of these?*
On the third night, it was silent 'til around 3 AM when
the gods cried together through my window.
They formed sections, argued about rules and tenets, threatened
to cut each other's branches or to send each other viruses and plagues.

Next morning, they started in about the nature of sin,
Some insisted there was no sin at all. Others made pronouncements
about the classification of sins:
deadly sins, mortal sins, venial sins. Perhaps sinners
could pay money to have all sin removed from their souls.
One said sins weren't sins if the right kind of person committed them.

A single god yelled out in a fantastic bellow...
You're wrong! I'm right! I know because I'm God!
Oh, they grew loud and shook my house to its very foundations.
I went to out to soothe them, *All right boys, where is the love?*
Be silent, woman! They hollered in unison.
And that was it.

I started to give them away like zucchini in fall.
I harvested them and baked them into pies.
What are you doing with us? One asked. *It hurts.*
See how you like it, I said.
I created my pièce de résistance in the kitchen.
Of course, I used extra butter and sugar, but I added
secret ingredients from an ancient family recipe,
I did the steps, I cast the incantations at the exact time,
and baked at just the right temperature.

When I say my pie was divine, oh, I mean it.
I sent pies out far and wide. One to the governor
and another to the pope.
I sent one to the president and all the judges supreme,
Here, I wrote, *have yourself a little sweet nothing.*
And all was good in the world.

You were not drinking in the kitchen
You weren't wobbling around the house in your boxer shorts
Your feet were not propped up on the table
A glass did not sweat in your hand
You did not crack skulls that day

So many times I've escaped. In dreams
I float through the house, my back almost
scraping the ceiling You never look up
The back door, open, behind where you sit like a guard
talking to yourself about your problems, the cost of things

Oh you would do the bit, playing all the monologues
you'd deliver to the shithead bosses and unruly women
You'd point and pause and drink and stammer and repeat
So many characters you contained so many voices
What would you have been without screwdrivers?

Somehow I willed you away that one day I came with a pink laundry
basket to an empty kitchen, the door open, no one to stop me,
All I had to do was remember how to fly. Almost too light to float
I'm a helium balloon. I'm a butterfly flitting, what iffing.
My wings won't catch at the threshold, but what about my sister?

Disown

refusal to acknowledge, and/ or maintain any connection with, people are often disowned by their family. to be disowned is to be ignored like you don't exist by a specific person/group, they act as if they don't know you, and never did. Synonyms: Deserted, ignored, isolated, jilted, marooned, cast off, friendless, Godforsaken, left behind, left in the lurch, lonely, thrown over, solitary, outcast.

slipped off easy like disintegrating gym shoes
you are a wind with no place to stop
a heart that won't keep time
ripe for anyone's picking
no one ever said you have a right
not to be abused
your original wound pulses beats
its rhythm never far from reach
takes a lifetime to mark in words
cast off like no one
ever named you
daughter

I wear the cross
my boyfriend gave me
after the first time
he took me to lover's lane.

I had pretended
I was in love.
Lust by itself
reserved for boys.

The cross cool against
bare neck, top of breasts molded
into wondrous cones studded silver
on black lace super uplift miracle bra.

The cross catches all
the light in the room, glints
belonging, vows protection
shows I'm taken.

My foster mother thinks
it obscene. She calls
the Mormon elders
who come for her

pineapple upside down cake,
to straighten me out,

to lay their hands.
Why would you wear the weapon that killed Christ?

They are inexplicably young,
these elders in ties tight as fists,
hair perfect golf course grass,
teeth straight up milk white bowling pins.

I'm all 80s in my high hair,
earrings I stole
out of her crystal chandelier.
So out of place

in the 70s ranch house
with the waterbed in the basement,
the tiny bedroom stuffed
with four other foster kids.

The power in me is strong,
vibrates out of my corset
all Joan Jet and Betty Davis.
I'm a redheaded Blondie.

I make them nervous.
These boy elders have never
been drunk, never sat in a steamy
car in the silken violet dark.

They beckon me to a chair
in the theater of the living room,
my foster family an audience propped
on stained velvet cushions.

Their eyes aglow with the spirit,
these hot Mormon elders
with prisons for morals.
This is no Catholic exorcism

no power of Christ compels, no removal
of my snakes. They try to put god in
my body by their supple perfect hands
on my back, head, throat, shoulders

30 minutes they shoot god
from their clean fingertips.
I sizzle full of the glory.
They ask if I believe.

Sweat drips from one of their plum mouths.
The blonde one tells me to choose.
The static between us
I can pretend is the lord,

but I know it's the animal
constrained tight beneath the twisted map of my freckles.
My oracle, the one who burns my lamp.
She says, *it's just a short while now. Hold on.*

WHEN THE SOCIAL WORKER TELLS ME NO
ONE WANTS A TEENAGE GIRL

I find many people want me,
men mostly on the T in the backs of their stores.
They say me I look so mature.
Madonna with a lace glove.
A chameleon like Boy George.
Wear the tips of all my heels.
Energy in my sinews I cannot contain.
It took me three tries and summer school
to pass trigonometry.
But I know how to add my value,
stalking Centre Street in my cheetah dress and my red heels.
I'm on the grand tour of foster homes. Eleven this year.
The corset from the Carousel at Lafayette Place
suits me like armor. My math is how many nights
I have free dinners and a place to stay.
Signing my own report cards, I hand them back to teachers,
dare them with my purple eyes from Revlon to question.
Who is it now, that one teacher in junior year
signs me up for SAT's without asking,
everyday wanting her $35 back.
The analogies on the test made no simple sense.
A girl is to the world,
what a mirror is to the sun.

When I look in the mirror I shake with my own power.
Oh, the costumes I endure to procure one night of value.
My friends might go to college, but they never
stopped a car dead in the middle of the city.
When doors open, I get in.

OF DOGS AND BOYS
(YOU KNOW HOW IT IS WITH DOGS)

There's a dog barking in the distance. I could know him.
I know all the dogs. You know how it is with dogs?
They want to be friends with the world. My dog,
loves the dead things he rolls in.
Burrows deep, his coat thick and oily
with the death stench. So proud he is to stink of rot.
You can't stop the way a dog is. He wears death,
a cloak of warning. A real dog
can't be contained.

So many sounds in the restless world. I'm
always listening out for threats and threats
of threats, threats within threats,
What is this knowing   how every living thing
has its unique rustling in branches, the fright of being
alone in nature in the dark out from inside a locked room

Once a man, really a boy, tried to strangle me in earth
in a dark corner of the park where I had walked freely with him.
At night. Then I felt in charge
of my own body, my own commander.
To him it seemed/ I mean to say/ he thought he heard me/ to him
it seemed I said *let anything be done* because he was listening

for anything that sounded like permission.

I thought I heard my own mind say, we won't die if we let it happen

Another part said *kick* said *run*
here in the night my feet pounding my heart
relentless woodpecker.
Keep going. Don't
stop. What if
this is my last night under
the terrible blinking eyes so neutral and fixed
watching us from the unmoving sky wall.

Not yet 18.
His hands
on my neck   Won't be the last
I can't hear you I can't hear you
Don't pretend.

The story ends all good because
an ancient woman's voice took over with
Stop, kick, hit, run.
Rip out his eyes with your thumbs.

What if I died
in the night
in the park

under the loveliness of trees
petals stuck
to the skin
I thought
A friend
Would never
Never would
A friend do that   to me
A secret enemy
Plotting to
Own me

He was weak and surprised
I was strong with
my shock kicked
my legs jumped, my heart,
out of the arboretum into the street
my clothes in sheets behind me his voice

I'll tell everyone you know!

The headlights spotlighting
the brakes screaming stopped
The driver a woman
Get in! Get in!
Her voice now the book of revelations:

What were you doing out in the night
in the dark alone in the park
with a boy

Don't you know boys are dogs
They aren't your friends
You can't   listen to anything they say,
her teeth tiny moons
in the closing red sky
of her firm, set mouth.

Post-Traumatic Growth

The positive psychological change some experience after traumatic events. Post-traumatic growth can yield unintentional positive changes in understanding self, relationships with others, personal strength, spirituality, and deeper appreciation of life and new possibilities.

MY ORACLE SAYS, A SELF-CENTO

I am the needle of your Golden Thread
receive my messages
you know you can swim through air
forget the skin borders
let the Word make you hum
glimmer in the knowing
with closed eyes that still see
hold the vision in its amber light
being alive is enough
you are to the world what a mirror is to the sun
all the blossoms bend to you
love is the star that always will wake you
You are free
so says the one who lights my lamp
I receive the messages
I send them back

WHEN I WAS A SINGLE MOTHER AND SOMEONE SPRAY-PAINTS A WALL AT UMASS: *GO HOME WELFARE CUNTS*

Erich Fromm saves my life,
tells me here is a system that people always enjoy.
Some like to inflict rules, some like to be told what to do.
This is a spectrum. Everyone is trying to escape from freedom.
Here all along I thought I was a bad girl.
Here I thought my choices made the world.

I try new ideas like a foal struggling to stand.
The one who claims to love me, comes home inebriated,
smelling like other people, doesn't care
a system exists that answers the question:
Why is he so violent?
He times my comings and goings.

My face, a clay mask, forms flexible smiles.
I bundle my child like a fragile package.
We step carefully around him, spilt out on the floor,
send ourselves out the door into the future. Is there
a place to time travel, a place without purple foodstamps
or his handprint on my throat?

My welfare worker tells me sociology is a useless degree.
It's for the rich to study us. I think of how they get to think

with full bellies and all that electricity.
Imagine them lit with knowledge,
lightning bugs with nothing to do but glimmer.
They have time to sit in comfortable chairs.
No belly rumble. No sick child. How I envy.
They sit and fully think all their thoughts,
write books telling the people about themselves.
They teach theory. They are called *professor.*

I think – *This is the land of opportunity!*
Go to the church, ask for food, beg
them to help keep my lights on,
promise I'll find their god.
I'll eat whatever they give me,
I'll sing their lying catechisms,
Be Not Afraid, they sing. But they don't
know who their god is.
Like my boyfriend, he forgives
if I repent, admit my guilt,
swear he is my one true divine.

The professors urge us to study
so we might change the world,
but they never get poverty right,
the tourists who write about us from afar
don costumes for an embedded welfare tour, credit card
an easy means of extraction always ready.

Fromm educates me about the system,
about those who wield power, those who suffer it.
He gives me a new vocabulary.
With new language I think new thoughts,
imagine possibilities of future worlds,
where I get to be a savior and write my own golden books.
In Sociology 101, I think I catch a glimpse.

Bruised bones, purple embers
Extinguished cigarettes
Singeing her scalp

Say what she's saying
laughing lighter than a collie
lashes waving and winking

She flirts a defense

Forgetting
Her voice in flight like bells
Echoing in wells

Emergency cash
Hot on her skin
No skulking or sneaking

She sang when she left
Waking the neighbors
Who doubted themselves

Back to sleep

Look for her
roots upon roots
Water under water

Her arms don't press in prayer to the sky

Replay her message
The laugh at the end
Capture it like a bird

THE BODY KEEPS SCORE ON WASH DAYS

You shake my hands
my laundry hanging
the line and the wheel keep their own rhythm
The towels and the sheets, oh the endless sheets
they hold in the sun
There is the spot the exact spot they kissed me
and there is the place I bled
but I keep the sheets because the thread count is high
I don't waste good money
The stain reveals dreams and memories
Who has so many beach towels, takes so many swims
Who has such large tables to cover

Your hands soothed as they hurt
I recall them holding me under water
Surely I would die
Why are you doing this
is it my mother or was it my sister
whose hands brushed my hair
cooked my eggs, corrected me
came with a towel wrapped me like a hug
I thought I won't open my eyes
I won't see   the towel with its stripes
so many pinks and oranges
a girl could get lost

You come to me in the bones
of my children, their faces so much
like yours, their necks long and elegant.
My own head squat against my shoulders
stunned by your return.
Your depression strives to live
in their exquisite bodies your memories.
Your burnings cry through them. I say it's the television
because I don't want to believe in you.
You come to me in dreams always in water
claiming me family.
I feel you waiting like a curve,
a nest some place that has always been mine.
My daughter tells me she is depressed.
I ask if she can change her mind.
I fear it's you planning your murders,
trying to get me through my children.
I make divine deals, I say take me not them.
I want to blame other people's parents
the TV, the social media,
screen time designed
to ruin them for money,
the toxic food and air.
I tell them don't eat suffering.

I warn them of the infection.
Don't bathe in dirty water,
I tell them, be like those three monkeys.
Develop foolproof mantras.
Imagine they are your bones.

Better not to return to my mother's old photo albums
where my possibility lies frozen like frogs under ice.

See me under the transparent film, light and rearrange my story,
those half-moon teeth, the dimming planets of my eyes.

I once believed I was as rock and fire as anything else,
instrumental as a rake or a wooden spoon.

The cast off articles of my faith- scapula, crucifix, rosary beads
in my lost memory box, replaced now with gull feathers, a collection

of stones gathered for their hand feel from my secret beach in Truro.
What I might have been. I let the sisters think I had the calling

when I wore the holy beads only to ward off vampires.
Arrange the photos, rearrange the timelines, the motivations.

See me there waiting, ready through the decades to spring to life,
my pulse could beat again if given a proper click, the correct kiss. CPR.

I once gave mouth to mouth to a dummy in 10th grade.
Took the gum out from my purple Madonna lips,
lace bow quivering in my hair,

laughed saying, *watch this*. I kissed the doll slowly til the teacher said,
Alright now....enough, left behind lipstick all waxy and shameless.

I sometimes imagine I am allowed to return, skip lanes, jump fates,
let my brother be the outcast.

Oh to be soothed by my mother's rough hand, to sit on her lap
of unfinished work.

Oh to be a golden petal pressed in her pages.

GHOSTS AND NEIGHBORS

My grandfather, Frank McDade
sold whiskey with his buddies during prohibition.
They called themselves *The Gustin Gang*.
But was this real or a Boston Irish tale like tumors
the size of watermelons, Great Uncle so and so
who swam the Boston Harbor island to island,
Aunts who aren't aunts. It was real
he served time at Deer Island,
Real he was a poet who wrote odes
to Boston and his wife who died in childbirth:

Yea, tho she rest beneath the graveyard sod, that ring is on her finger,
though her spirit rests with God.

And Grampy condemned his jailers:
I damn them all who sent me here, Deer Island Down the Bay.

I recall him only scary and untouchable
in his strange fedoras and rough smelly suits,
his wiry back straining to be upright.

There is a photo of him on the back deck of a Roxbury triple-decker,
laundry lines crisscross connecting homes behind him,
bony fists raised, poised to fight off ghosts and neighbors,

eyes focused on something hidden in the distance
over the shoulder of the photographer,
out of the picture maybe to a living room
where great grandchildren do their homework,
a family tree. Old lore and lines of his verse
are all I have to answer their questions,
to imagine who he was,
I pretend I knew him.

YOU VISIT MY SLEEP, MOTHER AND
SOMETIMES I AM NOT AFRAID

In the dream you see
how I came to be who I am
you allow it
in dreams it is easier to be kind
Your bones push through my face,
until I see you were there all along
I have the water and the words
I practice daily ablutions at the correct time
In the dream it is clear like salt
We dissolve into bruised and startling light
We rise like moons
With each task I bring you with me
I say you are worthy of love or something close to it
Your bones sigh in me
We bruise like plums
eat pain delicious
We call each other home

Out the window the bones of trees sway against a purple waiting sky.
I see my reflection. Folds of skin like rings in trees, tell my age.
I've disguised myself as a middle-aged mother.
Tonight, I sneak out to admire the trees I have visited for years.
Like old friends they remind me of oaths I made
in the secret clubhouse of childhood.
Cold air burns my lungs. Smoke of scotch and longing.
I imagine the trees speak to me in my mother's voice,
They say things like, *there is no devil greater than the devil in you.*
I pretend I hear them laugh.

I'd like to say she said,
It's an honor to live to see your own daughter through menopause.
She actually said: Just wait-
'til you get to see your own daughter go through it,
joy dancing in her eyes, sunlight on water.
She enjoyed her daughters' suffering.
She wanted me to have that, too.

I have these tricks of pretending one thing is another.

The doctor asked me the day of my last cycle.
Could I be a naturally pregnant 54 year old?
More likely you'd be hit by a Mack truck, how about a bus?
He hooted, slapped his own knee.

Am I not still full of surprises?
Don't all the flowers blossom and bend to me as I pass?

The last time I washed my daughter's honey hair,
I didn't know it was the last.
I should have lingered.
Should have sat in the Red Tent when I still had an invitation,
sucked bursting grapes from the pliable fingers of tent boys.

An unknown woman
showed me how to use a tampon,
in that long ago public bathroom,
my terror shaking the stalls, my shame just
about able to swallow us both.

My mother gave me a little pink book,
an old fashioned belt with 7 attachable pads
Any questions, she dared. Her fists tight, unopened buds.

Mother of the blue black hair and the midnight stare,
it was impolite to ask were you awake when I was born.
My mother, cold as milk, did you breastfeed?
Was dad good then?
When you made me, did God tell you the secret?

When I was 12 and suddenly
wanted to devour boys,
I was sure it was Satan
come down to take me.
I don't care. I don't care.
I begged. I implored.
I bathed my feet in oil for hours.
Come on, lead me astray.
Tell me the name of each living thing.

PRAISE BE MY BODY

How many times have I told my hands thank you?
When I say I love myself, I mean my creaky bones that ache and bend.
I mean this skin with its maps and marks.
It holds me in, shows where I've been.

So many times I wanted to shed this body that made me such a home,
a church for all the human doings. Thank you, body. I adore you.
You fed my three babies, each for a year.
How did I ever dare denigrate you?

When is the last time I told my neck, I am in awe of you?
How well you turn so I can breathe when I swim.
When did I last thank my eyes for their ways of finding exits.
What about elbows? How lucky to have them. How sweet to bend.

These legs that carry me. Oh my own solid thighs.
Magnificent feet, carry me in all directions. Thank you, feet.
Thank you belly and back that has been both beast and bridge .
I know you hurt. How I love you and your spine that holds me upright.

Body, I have hid in you before. Body, I have denied you,
spent weeks and months and years flaying away at you.
Show me what hurts. I will listen to your pain.
Take up all the space you need.

I will take you to our favorite places, the woods and the beach,
the town pool where my children laugh and joy lights their faces,
where I jump in and race the lifeguards, where I slowly exhale
all my air, lie on my back at the bottom of the pool without moving.

When I finally come up for air and my kids gather round
saying mama, how'd you do that?
All you do is let out all your air and let your body drop.
It's easy. I tell them. *Let me show you.*

THE MOTHERS OF DORCHESTER BAY

And we shall have a new bible,
and the holy name shall be Woman.
The colleges shall be made free.
The classrooms will burst open onto Morrissey Boulevard
and the streets and the monuments shall be renamed.
Research shall resume there
where our mothers' names were removed.
Their dreams once tread upon shall be made new and gleaming,
snapping like sheets in the wind,
strung tight between triple-deckers.
They shall go no more to priests
who devour their sons for being so sweet.
No more shall we be divided into parishes and projects.
My holy mother, St. Joan McDade shall be resurrected and redeemed.
Yes, the mothers of Dorchester Bay
shall float and rise like new Jesus.
All of Boston shall know their stories.
They shall live forever.
Bodies unblemished.
Eyes unblackened.

ACKNOWLEDGEMENTS

My gratitude to the following journals in which these poems (sometimes in slightly altered versions) first appeared:

Anti-Heroin Chic, "Praise Be My Body"

City Of Notions, an Anthology of Contemporary Boston Poems, "Dorchester Bike Ride"

(Published originally as Vodka, Beer, and Cigarettes)

City Of Notions, an Anthology of Contemporary Boston Poems, "Dot Girl"

Lily Poetry Review, "Closest to God"

Muddy River Poetry Review, "Where the Water Meets the Sky"

Nixes Mate Review, "Uncle Hugh"

The MacGuffin, "My Mother's Eyes Were Birds"

The MacGuffin, "When the Social Worker Tells Me No one Wants a Teenage Girl"

The MacGuffin, "Grand Climacteric"

spoKe, "God Tree"

Hiedra | Revista Electrónica de Literatura (Mexico), translated By María Del Castillo Sucerquia, "Where the Water Meets the Sky" and "Your Golden Thread".

Bohemia Caribe: Literatura Internacional(Columbia), translated by María Del Castillo Sucerquia, "Uncle Hugh", "Mother's Day", and "Sister Why Must Our Saviors Bleed Forever".

Read Carpet, (Columbia), Translated by María Del Castillo Sucerquia, "Dot Girl" and "Praise Be My Body".

"Dot Girl" was a winner of the 2017 Boston Mayor's Poetry Program, judged by Poet Laureate Danielle Legros Georges. Displayed at Boston City Hall.

"Vodka, Beer and Cigarettes" was a winner of the 2017 Boston Mayor's Poetry Program, judged by Poet Laureate Danielle Legros Georges. Displayed at Boston City Hall.

"Tinean Beach" (Published in this collection as "Where the Water Meets the Sky")was a winner of the 2018 Boston Mayor's Poetry Program, judged by Poet Laureate Danielle Legros Georges. Displayed at Boston City Hall.

"Ghosts and Neighbors" was a winner of the 2019 Boston Mayor's Poetry Program, judged by Poet Laureate Porsha Olayiwola. Displayed at Boston City Hall.

"St Joan McDade The Resurrected and Redeemed" (Published in the collection as "The Mothers of Dorchester Bay") was a winner of the 2020 Boston Mayor's Poetry Program, judged by Poet Laureate Porsha Olayiwola. "Praise Be My Body" was a runner-up of the 2023 Boston Mayor's Poetry Program, judged by Poet Laureate Porsha Olayiwola.

Thank you to the Boston Mayor's Office of Arts and Culture for awarding me an Artist Opportunity Grant in 2022, which enabled me to attend the Marge Piercy Writing Workshop, Workshop with Gloria Monaghan at Castle Hill, and the Lily Poetry Review Manuscript Intensive, all of which I am so grateful for, all of which made the work of writing, editing, and crafting of this manuscript possible.

Thank you to the many poets and teachers in my community who believed in my work and encouraged me to write including, Danielle Legros Georges, Eileen Cleary, Alexis Ivy, Marge Piercy and my Piercy workshop cohorts, Tom Daly and the folks in the Monday night workshop, Matthew Henry, and Lindsey O'Neill. I am very grateful to Anne Pluto and Michael McInnis for seeing something in my work and requesting the manuscript. I so appreciate the unyielding support of my husband, David Goodrich and our children, Philip, Isabelle, and Graham. My mother-in-law, Marilyn Goodrich was a source of continued encouragement, even when I was most doubtful. Thanks to Jim Michmerhuizen whose wonderful workshops on true speech and the essence of poetry got me back into writing after many years on hiatus raising children. Thank you to my mentor Deborah Leipziger for continued guidance and support and to Max Regan for helping me with edits and confidence. My eternal gratitude to Kay, Caroline and Connie for showing me the way.

There are some people who saved my young spirit in ways they probably did not know. They are most definitely why I'm alive: Irene Collins who was the youth choir director at St Ann's Church, Mrs. Murphy who created and coached a neighborhood track team and brought all the girls to our first road races including the Bonnie Bell, Carl Cederquist who coached the Greater Boston Swim Club, Dr. Robert Binswanger, Headmaster of Boston Latin Academy who helped me the best he could when I was in foster care, my tenth grade English teacher, Mrs. Thompson who told me she saw gold in my writing, and Max the neighborhood German Shephard who truly was my best friend. In the very least, I owe them poems, but here they have my deepest gratitude and recognition.

ABOUT THE AUTHOR

Linda Carney-Goodrich is a writer and teacher from Boston. Her work has appeared in *spoKe, Lily Poetry Review, The MacGuffin, Nixes Mate Review, Anti-Heroin Chic, Literary Mama, Muddy River Poetry Review, Wordgathering Journal of Disability Poetry and Literature, Gyroscope Review, Songs of Eretz Poetry Review*, and *City of Notions: An Anthology of Contemporary Boston Poems*. Her work has been translated in Columbia and Mexico. Over the years several poems of hers have been displayed on the walls at Boston City Hall as part of the Boston Mayor's Poetry Program judged by the Boston Poet Laureate. Linda is the Poetry Coordinator for the Menino Art Center in Hyde Park and owner of Home Scholars of Boston. She earned a Master's in Education from Harvard Graduate School of Education and a Bachelor of Science degree in Human Services from Springfield College of Human Services. Her one person shows include *The Secret Childhood Diary of a Welfare Mother* and *My Life in Barbie. Dot Girl* is her first collection of poetry. See more at lindacarneygoodrich.com

42° 19' 47.9" N 70° 56' 43.9" W

Nixes Mate is a navigational hazard in Boston Harbor used during the colonial period to gibbet and hang pirates and mutineers.

Nixes Mate Books features small-batch artisanal literature, created by writers who use all 26 letters of the alphabet and then some, honing their craft the time-honored way: one line at a time.

nixesmate.pub

Printed in the USA
CPSIA information can be obtained
at www.ICGtesting.com
CBHW030739130224
4201CB00006B/5